Thea Howorth
Poppies 'Moving On'
Celebration
July 2023

For Tilda

To receive a current seed catalogue, please contact Thompson & Morgan on 01473 601090

First published in the United Kingdom in 1999 by Ragged Bears Publishing Limited, Milborne Wick, Sherborne, Dorset DT9 4PW

Distributed by Ragged Bears Limited, Ragged Appleshaw, Andover, Hampshire SP11 9HX. Tel: 01264 772269

A CIP record of this book is available from the British Library

ISBN 1 85714 180 6

Printed in Singapore

Tilda's Seeds

Melanie Eclare

Ragged Bears Publishing
Produced in association with **Thompson & Morgan**

Tilda loves growing sunflowers.

These are the seeds she bought with her pocket money.

The best time to start growing
sunflowers is in the spring,
so in March, Tilda begins to dig.

She prepares a flowerbed
by clearing the weeds and
then making a hole for
each seed. Then, she takes
the seeds out of the
packet.

Thompson & Morgan
SUNFLOWER
CONTENTS 40 SEEDS
HARDY A

Thomp
SUNFLOWER

Tilda pulls all the seeds out of the old flower.

Now she has her own
sunflower seeds to grow
for next year.